A LOOK AT LIFE SCIENCE

WHAT ARE ANIMALS?

BY KATE MIKOLEY

Gareth Stevens
PUBLISHING

Please visit our website, www.garethstevens.com. For a free color catalog of all our high-quality books, call toll free 1-800-542-2595 or fax 1-877-542-2596.

Library of Congress Cataloging-in-Publication Data

Names: Mikoley, Kate, author.
Title: What are animals? / Kate Mikoley.
Description: New York : Gareth Stevens Publishing, [2020] | Series: A look at life science | Includes index.
Identifiers: LCCN 2019012447| ISBN 9781538248430 (paperback) | ISBN 9781538248454 (library bound) | ISBN 9781538248447 (6 pack)
Subjects: LCSH: Animals--Juvenile literature.
Classification: LCC QL49 .M6185 2020 | DDC 590--dc23
LC record available at https://lccn.loc.gov/2019012447

First Edition

Published in 2020 by
Gareth Stevens Publishing
111 East 14th Street, Suite 349
New York, NY 10003

Copyright © 2020 Gareth Stevens Publishing

Designer: Reann Nye
Editor: Kate Mikoley

Photo credits: Series art MriMan/Shutterstock.com; cover Ondrej Prosicky/Shutterstock.com; p. 5 Nico Faramaz/Shutterstock.com; p. 7 Per-Gunnar Ostby/Photodisc/Getty Images; p. 9 Rich Carey/Shutterstock.com; p. 11 Olha Rohulya/Shutterstock.com; p. 13 DelmasLehman/iStock/Getty Images Plus/Getty Images; p. 15 Ethan Daniels/Shutterstock.com; p. 17 Regien Paassen/Shutterstock.com; p. 19 diana deak/Shutterstock.com; p. 21 Catherine Falls Commercial/Moment/Getty Images; p. 23 Sergey Uryadnikov/Shutterstock.com; p. 25 wim claes/Shutterstock.com; p. 27 JoannaPerchaluk/Shutterstock.com; p. 29 jn.koste/Shutterstock.com; p. 30 Andrew Paul Deer/Shutterstock.com.

All rights reserved. No part of this book may be reproduced in any form without permission in writing from the publisher, except by a reviewer.

Printed in the United States of America

Some of the images in this book illustrate individuals who are models. The depictions do not imply actual situations or events.

CPSIA compliance information: Batch #CW20GS: For further information contact Gareth Stevens, New York, New York at 1-800-542-2595.

CONTENTS

All About Animals	4
The Animal Kingdom	6
On the Move	8
How Did They Get Here?	14
What's for Dinner?	16
Brilliant Backbones	18
Many Mammals	20
Beautiful Birds	22
Staying Warm	24
Animal Adaptations	26
So Many Animals!	28
Classifying the Lion	30
Glossary	31
For More Information	32
Index	32

Words in the glossary appear in **bold** type the first time they are used in the text.

ALL ABOUT ANIMALS

You already know that the creatures you see at the zoo are animals. Your pets are animals, too. Even you—a human—are an animal! There's much more to know about the amazing **organisms** that make up the animal kingdom.

MAKE THE GRADE

Animals are sorted into groups. The broadest group is a kingdom. Within kingdoms are smaller groups called phylums, classes, orders, and families. An animal's most **specific** classifications are its genus and species.

THE ANIMAL KINGDOM

A kingdom is a grouping of organisms. All animals are part of the animal kingdom. Other living things, such as plants, have their own kingdoms. Let's see what makes animals different from organisms in other kingdoms!

MAKE THE GRADE

Animals are made up of many cells. Some organisms are made up of only one cell.

ON THE MOVE

To live, animals need food and water. They also need to breathe. Most animals have muscles. Muscles are body parts that help allow animals to move. Being able to move is key for staying alive in the animal world.

MAKE THE GRADE

Even fish breathe! They breathe through body parts called gills.

Unlike plants and some other living things, such as **fungi**, animals can move from place to place on their own. They commonly do this by walking, running, flying, or swimming. Animals also eat other living things, such as plants or other animals.

MAKE THE GRADE
Being able to move is important for animals, so they can find food and water **sources**.

Animals can change their behavior, or the way they act, based on things happening around them. For example, if a deer sees a predator nearby, the deer may use its speed to run away. Plants can't do this!

MAKE THE GRADE

Some kinds of deer can run about 40 miles (64 km) per hour for short amounts of time!

HOW DID THEY GET HERE?

The animals we see in the world today haven't always been around. Scientists think animals **evolved** from single-celled organisms that lived in the sea. Around 350 million years ago, they moved to **habitats** on land and in freshwater.

MAKE THE GRADE

Not all animals have arms and legs—or even faces! Sponges are animals that, for a long time, were mistakenly thought to be plants!

WHAT'S FOR DINNER?

Different animals often have very different **diets**. Animals that eat other animals are called carnivores. Examples of carnivores include wolves and lions. Animals that eat only plants are herbivores. Elephants, zebras, and rabbits are all herbivores.

MAKE THE GRADE

An animal that eats both plants and animals is an omnivore. Some animals commonly thought of as carnivores, such as bears, are actually omnivores because they eat plants, too.

BRILLIANT BACKBONES

Animals are sorted into two basic groups: vertebrates, or those with a backbone, and invertebrates, or those without a backbone. A backbone, also called a spine, is a row of bones that protects the animal's **spinal cord**.

MAKE THE GRADE

More than 90 percent of animal species, or kinds, alive today are invertebrates! These include jellyfish and earthworms.

MANY MAMMALS

There are five main groups of vertebrates. These are fish, **amphibians**, birds, **reptiles**, and mammals. A mammal is a **warm-blooded** vertebrate with hair. They feed milk to their young and breathe air. Mammal brains are more developed, or advanced, than many other animals.

MAKE THE GRADE

Humans are mammals! So are cats, elephants, dolphins, and many other animals.

BEAUTIFUL BIRDS

Like mammals, birds are warm-blooded vertebrates. Unlike mammals, though, birds have feathers and wings. Most birds can use their wings to fly around. However, even though all birds have wings, some kinds, such as penguins, can't fly!

MAKE THE GRADE
At one time, penguins could fly. But scientists have found that as their wings evolved to help them swim better, penguins lost the ability to fly.

STAYING WARM

Reptiles, amphibians, and most fish are cold-blooded vertebrates. Their blood isn't always cold. Their body **temperature** depends on how warm or cold the air or water around them is. Invertebrates are cold-blooded animals, too.

MAKE THE GRADE
Cold-blooded animals may stay in sunny areas to keep warm.

25

ANIMAL ADAPTATIONS

A change that helps an animal live better in its **environment** is called an adaptation. Penguins' wings being helpful for swimming is an adaptation. Arctic foxes' white fur is an adaptation that helps them blend in with snow and hide from predators.

MAKE THE GRADE
Many animals, including arctic foxes, grow thicker fur to stay warm in cold temperatures.

SO MANY ANIMALS!

It's hard to know exactly how many animals live on our planet. Scientists have been able to **identify** nearly 2 million different species of animals, but there are likely many more. It's possible there are millions we don't yet know about!

MAKE THE GRADE

Scientists sort animals into groups, such as family and species, based on features they have in common. This is called classifying.

CLASSIFYING THE LION

KINGDOM
animals

PHYLUM
vertebrates

CLASS
mammals

ORDER
carnivores

FAMILY
cats

GENUS
big cats

SPECIES
lions

GLOSSARY

amphibian: an animal that spends time on land but must have babies and grow into an adult in water

diet: the food an animal eats

environment: the conditions that surround a living thing and affect the way it lives

evolve: to grow and change over time

fungi: living things that are somewhat like plants but don't make their own food, have leaves, or have a green color

habitat: the natural place where an animal or plant lives

identify: to find out the name or features of something

organism: a living thing

reptile: an animal covered with scales or plates that breathes air, has a backbone, and lays eggs

source: something that offers a supply of a particular thing

specific: precise or exact

spinal cord: a thick rope of nerve tissue extending from the brain

temperature: how hot or cold something is

warm-blooded: able to keep the body at a steady temperature no matter what the outside temperature is

FOR MORE INFORMATION

BOOKS

Booth, Edison. *Animals and Their Environments*. New York, NY: PowerKids Press, 2017.

Dunne, Abbie. *Animal Group Behavior*. North Mankato, MN: Capstone Press, 2017.

WEBSITES

Animals
www.ducksters.com/animals.php
This website has fascinating facts about all sorts of animals.

Classifying Animals
www.dkfindout.com/us/animals-and-nature/animal-kingdom/classifying-animals/
Learn more about how animals are classified here.

Publisher's note to educators and parents: Our editors have carefully reviewed these websites to ensure that they are suitable for students. Many websites change frequently, however, and we cannot guarantee that a site's future contents will continue to meet our high standards of quality and educational value. Be advised that students should be closely supervised whenever they access the internet.

INDEX

adaptation 26
animal kingdom 4, 5, 6
carnivore 16, 17, 30
class 5, 30
classification 5, 30
family 5, 29, 30
genus 5, 30
habitat 14
herbivore 16
invertebrate 18, 19, 24
omnivore 17
order 5, 30
organism 4, 6, 7, 14
phylum 5, 30
species 5, 19, 28, 29, 30
vertebrate 18, 20, 22, 24, 30